BRAD MARCHAND

BRAD MARCHAND

THE UNLIKELY STAR

PHILIP CROUCHER

Foreword by Andrew Brickley,
Boston Bruins analyst

NIMBUS
PUBLISHING
— NIMBUS.CA —

Nimbus Publishing Limited
3660 Strawberry Hill Street, Halifax, NS, B3K 5A9
(902) 455-4286 nimbus.ca

Printed and bound in Canada

NB1325

Editor: Elaine McCluskey
Design: Jenn Embree

Library and Archives Canada Cataloguing in Publication

Croucher, Philip, author
Brad Marchand : the unlikely star / Philip Croucher.
ISBN 978-1-77108-685-1 (softcover)

1. Marchand, Brad, 1989-. 2. Hockey players—Canada—Biography. I. Title.

GV848.5.M365C76 2018   796.962092   C2018-902868-8

Nimbus Publishing acknowledges the financial support for its publishing activities from the Government of Canada, the Canada Council for the Arts, and from the Province of Nova Scotia. We are pleased to work in partnership with the Province of Nova Scotia to develop and promote our creative industries for the benefit of all Nova Scotians.

CONTENTS

FOREWORD

HAVING GROWN UP IN BOSTON, spent four of my twelve NHL seasons playing in a Boston Bruins uniform, and now in my second decade serving as colour analyst for Boston Bruins telecasts on the New England Sports Network, I have a unique perspective of the dynamic, yet controversial, fan favourite Brad Marchand.

The Bruins had the makings of a dynasty in the early 1970s. Stanley Cup winners in 1970 and again in 1972. They had the greatest player in the history of the game in Bobby Orr, future hall of famers Phil Esposito and Johnny Bucyk, and talented players with large personalities like Derek Sanderson, Johnny McKenzie, and Gerry Cheevers.

These guys were my idols. My generation of aspiring local youth hockey players all dreamed of playing in the NHL and donning a Bruins jersey.

What a "gang" they were. The Bruins had swagger; they were swashbucklers, immensely popular, and visible around town. More importantly, they were hard-working and accountable, to go along with their tremendous skill. Imagine being a Bruin and winning the Stanley Cup.

But that dynasty never materialized. In fact, what followed was a thirty-nine-year drought. The Don Cherry teams of the late 1970s couldn't beat the Montreal Canadiens, and the Ray Bourque/Cam Neely era—

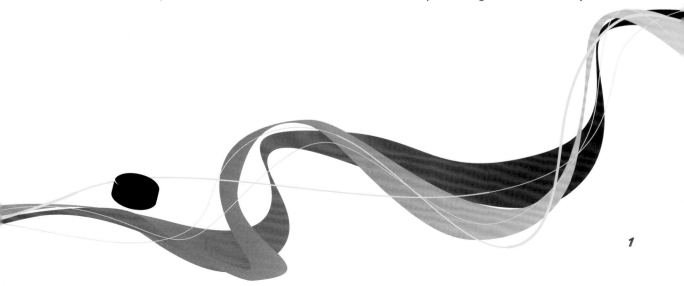

my seasons in Boston—lost the final in both 1988 and 1990.

But that all changed in 2011. To have been a part of that team, to have experienced that journey of total sacrifice and commitment and what it meant to not only the players and the organization but to the fan base, was truly special.

Ah...memories. That 2011 team had a new generation of heroes: Tim Thomas, Zdeno Chára, Patrice Bergeron, Mark Recchi, Nathan Horton, and the "Little Ball of Hate," Brad Marchand.

When Marchand first appeared on the scene in Boston, he looked like a player who had a chance to be an effective bottom-six forward, potential penalty-killer, and he certainly had the reputation of a "pest." He could take the best of opponents off their game by being a borderline trash-talking, dirty player.

But if you talked to Brad, he was convinced he was much more than that. He felt he had much more to offer and that he could "score twenty goals a season in this league."

Don't you just love athletes who prove themselves right? Not with arrogance but with a hardened self-belief that comes from family values and overcoming the challenges of people putting artificial limits on your abilities early in life.

Marchand is a star in the National Hockey League, and to be able to watch him play and compete—and I mean *compete*—game in and game out, makes you wish every player had his inner drive.

What impresses me the most has been his maturation process. Despite the fines and suspensions, and his continued "playing on the edge," Marchand has great respect for the game, his teammates, and his opponents.

Will he ever be "broken in"? Doubtful, but he feels in order to be the player he is, he needs to play a certain way.

As a colour analyst, what's admirable to me is Marchand's understanding of the value of a two-hundred-foot game. The realization that the puck is the most important aspect of the game of hockey. The ability to protect it when you have it, the relentless pursuit when you need it back, and each time you move it, it's done with purpose.

Combine that approach to the game with his skill, his will to win, and his team-first attitude, and you have a phenomenal player.

Marchand is a treasure in Boston. He takes us back to the Big Bad Bruins with his talent and bravado. He's helped create a new next generation of young hockey players who idolize the Bruins and proudly wear their black-and-gold number 63 jerseys.

There is no one blueprint on how to make it to the NHL and then to take that opportunity and become one of the best players in the game...but Marchand has done just that.

—Andrew Brickley, former NHL player, current TV analyst for Boston Bruins on New England Sports Network
April 2018

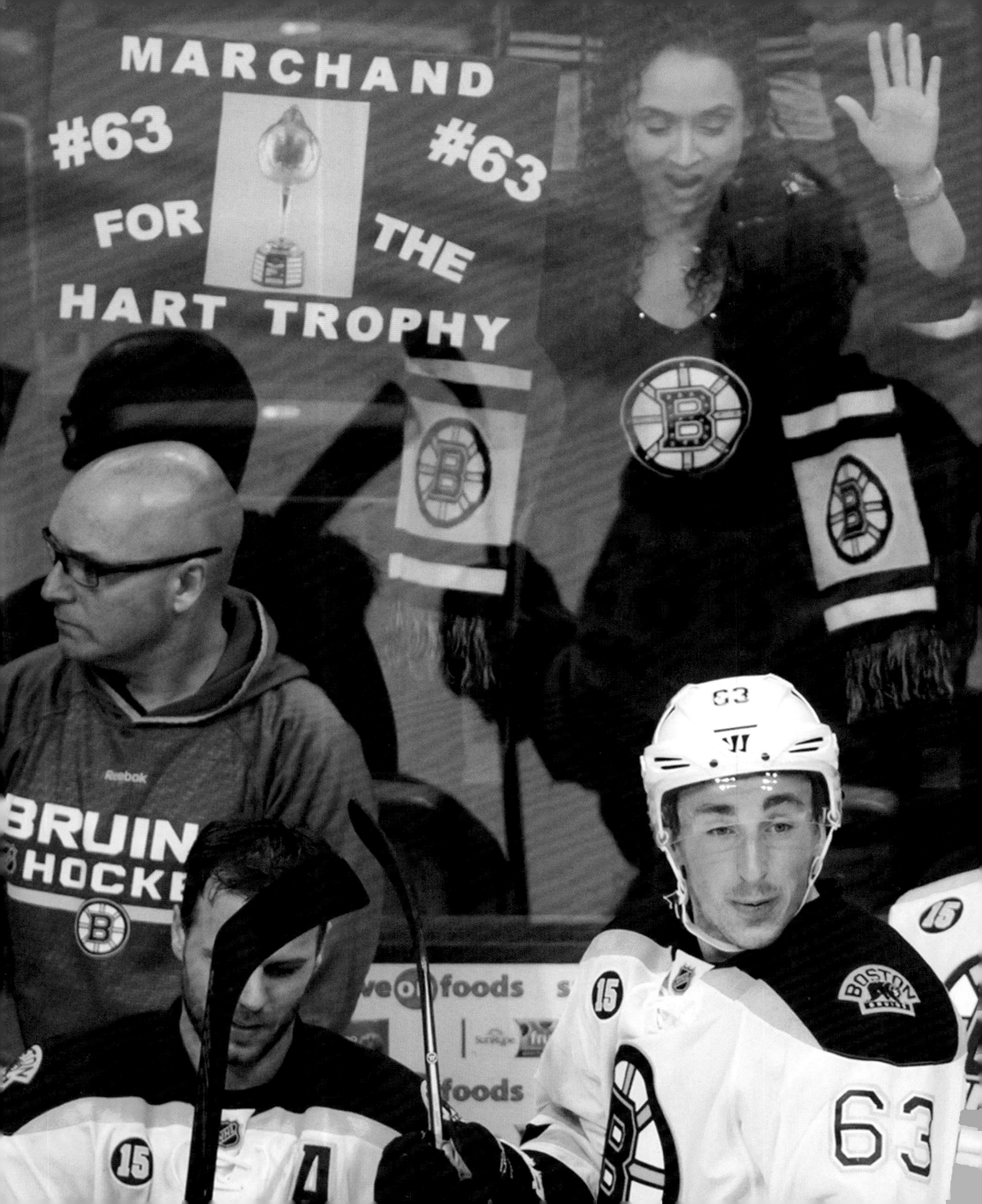
MARCHAND
#63
#63
FOR
THE
HART TROPHY
Reebok
63
BOSTON
63

INTRODUCTION

BRAD MARCHAND BEGAN TO reflect on his career as he gazed out the window of the airplane on a mid-October day in 2010. There was much to look back on.

From first donning the blades as a toddler, to his minor hockey days where he turned heads with a skill set and intensity few could match. Then there was being one of the last players to make the Nova Scotia Major Midget Hockey League's Dartmouth Subways, only to then go and lead the elite squad in scoring. There was also winning a Quebec Major Junior Hockey League title, two gold medals for Team Canada at the World Junior Hockey Championships, and of course, getting drafted by the NHL's Boston Bruins.

But at this moment, it paled in comparison to the feeling he was experiencing. He had just finished playing his first two NHL games of the season for the Bruins in the Czech Republic and was heading back to Boston on a ten-hour flight. He had gone overseas for the rare regular-season NHL games, not knowing if he would make the team or get sent down again to the American Hockey League after returning home.

These were stressful times in his hockey world. But Marchand was finally able to stop worrying. Before that first game against the Phoenix Coyotes, he had been told that he had made the Bruins. Brad Marchand was in the opening-day lineup.

A fan holds up a sign behind Brad Marchand after he scored a goal in Vancouver in 2017. The sign reflects his popularity with Bruins fans.
(DARRYL DYCK, THE CANADIAN PRESS)

"I couldn't believe that I made the NHL," he remembers thinking on that flight back to Boston. "Having that confidence and being a part of that opening-day roster, it made me feel comfortable [and] that I belonged, that I deserved to be there. I think I just got more confident every day I stepped onto the ice."

Fast-forward almost ten years and Marchand is now an NHL superstar. He's also one of the most controversial players in the league. Fast, highly skilled, and incredibly driven, the Hammonds Plains, Nova Scotia, forward is one of the top scorers in the NHL. He's also one of the most hated by opponents and some fans.

Marchand plays on the edge. Sometimes, he goes too far. The infamous licking incidents during the 2018 Stanley Cup playoffs were, he concedes, a mistake. "I have to be a lot better." Otherwise, Marchand makes no apologies for how he plays—or the brash, at times cocky, persona he can give off.

"There's very little that can upset me," he says without hesitation when being interviewed for this book during the 2017–18 season. "I am doing what I love and doing it in the NHL. Where all the hate is coming from is because I am successful at what I do. It's a compliment when people don't like me or my game, because it means I'm doing something."

Marchand's story is inspiring for anyone told they aren't good enough. Too small, not enough skill, not enough speed—Marchand heard it all growing up. Yet he's the one vindicated because he took that criticism—sometimes fair, sometimes not—and used it to push himself harder and harder to get where he is.

"That's what we brought up our kids to believe," his father, Kevin, says. "You can go through a wall and do whatever you want. There's no limit. So set your dreams high."

Marchand has developed into one of the top-five hockey players Nova Scotia has ever produced. After Cole Harbour's Sidney Crosby and Port Hood's Al MacInnis, you could argue, in fact, there's been no one better.

I'd like to thank Andy Brickley for writing the book's foreword. I'd also like to thank Brad Marchand and his family for being so open for this book and allowing me to tell his story in such great detail.

Marchand also isn't afraid to speak his mind, which helped make this book so much fun to write. I hope you enjoy reading his story. I know I enjoyed telling it to you.

EARLY YEARS

THE CAN-DO ATTITUDE OF BRAD Marchand came at an early age. His father, Kevin, smiles telling the story of how, at two and a half, his son demanded that the training wheels be taken off his bicycle.

"'No, Brad, you are going to hurt yourself,'" Kevin recalls telling him.

Brad was adamant. He wanted them off. He was doing this.

"So I took them off—and he had to use the curb to get on the bike. The moment he got on, he knew it and he drove away.

He had no hesitation. It was a bit of his own self-awareness and confidence to challenge himself to do it."

Marchand faced challenges like this often as a minor hockey player, and he always succeeded. Growing up in Hammonds Plains in an upscale, quiet neighbourhood outside Halifax, Marchand was always one of the best players on the team he suited up for in the TASA minor-hockey system. But he was never that can't-miss prospect like fellow local stars Sidney Crosby and Nathan MacKinnon,

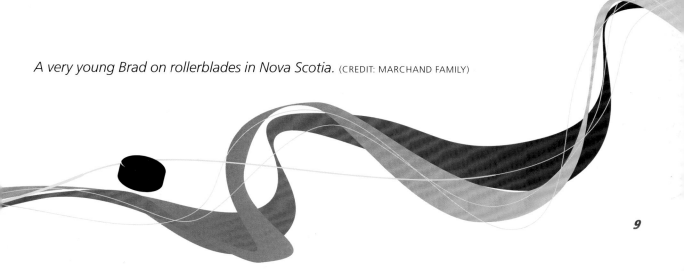

A very young Brad on rollerblades in Nova Scotia. (CREDIT: MARCHAND FAMILY)

Young Brad was always anxious to get to the rink. (CREDIT: MARCHAND FAMILY)

Was Marchand very good? Absolutely. Not many minor hockey players can tally more than 90 goals and 150 points while playing bantam AAA. Was he destined for the NHL like everyone said Crosby was? That remained to be seen.

"I think we all dreamed of it, we all wanted to do it, but in no way was he a prodigy at that age," says close friend Andrew Bodnarchuk.

Bodnarchuk was thirteen when he moved to Hammonds Plains with his family from out west and has since gone on to have a successful professional career himself, with over forty NHL games, including five with the Bruins, sixteen with the Columbus Blue Jackets, and twenty-one with the Colorado Avalanche. He played the 2017–18 season with the American Hockey League's Texas Stars.

"If you look at Nathan [MacKinnon] or Sidney [Crosby], they kind of had that hype where they were destined to go to the NHL. I think that benefitted Brad in a way. It's something he wanted to do, but he knew it was something he had to work at," recalls Bodnarchuk.

Marchand loved the game and never needed a push to play. On many Saturday mornings, Marchand was so ready to be at

in the years before and after him. Crosby is nine months older than Marchand, and the two lived on opposite sides of the Halifax region and played in different hockey circles. They knew of each other, of course, but the comparisons stopped there.

Brad Marchand was never shy talking about one day playing in the NHL. It's something he spoke about regularly with his parents and any friends willing to listen.

Lynn remembers when he was in grade seven and she walked into his bedroom one night and saw her son's name scribbled over and over again on a piece of loose-leaf.

"Side to side, top to bottom, both pages, completely filled with him just practising his autograph," she laughs. "I said, 'What are you doing?' He said, 'I'm practising my autograph for when I make the NHL.' It was so cool because in grade seven, he thought, *because I'm going to make the NHL, I better practise my signature.*"

A hockey photo of Brad from 1996.
(CREDIT: MARCHAND FAMILY)

practice or games that he would have his parents waiting in the parking lot before the rink was open.

"He loved hockey the first time he put on skates," his mother, Lynn, says. "The passion was always there."

Lynn is a schoolteacher while Kevin runs his own building company for new homes in suburban Halifax. Kevin was a good hockey player in his own right,

making it to the university level. The family of six includes Brad's brother, Jeff, and sisters, Melissa and Rebecca, all of whom are younger. When it came to their older son and his on-ice skill, Kevin and Lynn offered support and, when needed, straight talk on his journey to be the best.

One thing Brad heard often in minor hockey was that he wasn't big enough, or skilled enough to make it. He is listed at

Brad Marchand and Andrew Bodnarchuk were best friends and teammates while growing up. Shown here as juniors with the Canadian flag. Both were drafted by Boston.
(CREDIT: MARCHAND FAMILY)

five foot nine and 180 pounds, but was smaller in minor hockey. His height was something many critics used as the reason he would never make the NHL, which was more of a big-man's game at the time. He heard this from everyone—coaches, friends—even some within his distant family.

"It drove me a lot to be better," Marchand says. "I think I had a lot of people in my corner, pushing me the [right] way. My family was huge for that—pumping me up, almost to false expectations. They told me I was that good, and you started to believe it a bit—that you can do it.

"The more people harp that you are not good enough, or they are more concerned about guys that are ahead of you—they give all the attention to different guys—it just made me want to push that much harder… The more people kind of doubted, the more I wanted to throw it in their face. I got a lot of pleasure [in that]. I was very happy to be able to do that. It was a good feeling."

It was by peewee that Kevin really noticed his son might have what it takes to play professionally. He had good speed and a skill set few could stop, but maybe more importantly there was a competiveness and a desire to win, at any cost.

"The will to win the battles to the puck, the will to win the battles out of the corner, win the battles to score goals. Few players have that capability to get those clutch goals, and he started to do that in peewee," Kevin says.

Marchand really put his name on the local hockey map at the midget AAA level. The Dartmouth Subways have a long and storied history in the Nova Scotia Major Midget Hockey League. In the early 2000s, it was the team most elite players in the Halifax region wanted to be on. Going into the 2003–04 season, future first-round-NHL-draft-choice James Sheppard, along with his close friend

Dartmouth Subways all-time top points per season (according to elite-prospects.com):

- Sidney Crosby (2001–02): 74G, 95A, 193P

- Andrew Joudrey (2000–01): 51G, 70A, 121P

- Brad Marchand (2003–04): 47G, 47A, 94P

- James Sheppard (2003–04): 38G, 54A, 92P

- Blake Gallaher (2004–05): 38G, 39A, 77P

Ryan Hillier, were the team's biggest recruits.

Marchand also wanted to be on the club but unlike Sheppard and Hillier, his spot wasn't a sure thing. Going into the August tryouts, his father remembers there were three spots available. Marchand, along with his good friend Bodnarchuk, earned two of them.

"He had to work his butt off to achieve that goal," Kevin says of his son. "It was a war out there to earn those spots."

Marchand showed his value to the Subways and, in the process, took his game to another level. By season's end he finished with 47 goals—94 points—and

A teenaged Marchand during his early hockey days in Nova Scotia. (CREDIT: MARCHAND FAMILY)

led the Subways in scoring. It's also the third-most points ever recorded in any season by a Subways player. Not bad for someone earning one of the last spots on the team. You can probably guess who is number one.

"There were always other guys who were more highly touted, but it also allowed me to kind of sit in the weeds a bit," Marchand says of that season with Dartmouth. "A lot of the top guys kind of fade off at some point when they don't have to work as hard to get to the next level. Where when you have to bust your butt to make a certain team, of if you have to do a little more than everyone else, that's the backbone to a lot of guys that do well over time. Not just make it—but sustain it and have a long career."

Brad Marchand came home to a hero's welcome at the Halifax airport after winning gold for Canada at the World Juniors. (CREDIT: MARCHAND FAMILY)

His strong play with Dartmouth was also getting him noticed by QMJHL scouts. Growing up a fan of the Halifax Mooseheads, Marchand wanted his next step in hockey to be at the major junior level. When the QMJHL draft rolled around in June 2004, Marchand was considered a potential first-round pick.

He didn't go in the first round, but he did go high—twenty-fourth overall and in the second round—to the Moncton Wildcats.

It was time for his next challenge in hockey. He was ready.

JUNIOR DAYS

GOING INTO HIS FIRST CAMP with the Wildcats, Marchand's goal was simple: make the team. As a high draft pick his chances were good, but he still needed to show he was ready to make the jump after one year of midget.

Like with the Subways a year earlier, Marchand landed one of the final spots with Moncton at training camp. He was thrilled and would be playing close to home, as the New Brunswick team was located only about a three-hour drive from Hammonds Plains. But Marchand was about to learn that ice time at the junior level was more difficult to get.

"I think he only played in six of his first ten games. That was tough," Kevin says. "There was uncertainty about how he was going to be utilized. That took some patience—going from a major contributor on the Subways program to the next level, where you are playing against twenty-one year olds and you have to filter into that group."

Marchand, then sixteen, quickly adapted and began to show a more well-rounded game.

Marchand had to prove himself with the Moncton Wildcats. (CREDIT: DANIEL ST LOUIS)

The Hockey News Scouting Report on Brad Marchand:

ASSETS

Owns very good scoring instincts and hockey sense. Is a world-class agitator and sparkplug type who plays way bigger than his 5-9 frame suggests. Is effective on special teams. Confident with the puck, he produces in the clutch.

FLAWS

Plays over the edge sometimes. Size can be an issue at the National Hockey League level, especially because of his annoying style of play (he draws plenty of attention from opponents). Injuries may be a concern down the road.

CAREER POTENTIAL

Excellent scoring winger and agitator.

Team headshot when Marchand was playing with Val-d'Or in the QMJHL.
(CREDIT: VAL-D'OR FOREURS)

He started the season on the fourth line and would kill penalties and bring important energy. He also contributed offensively. By the second half of the season, his ice time had grown and he was becoming a key offensive threat.

"He seems to have a real knack to be able to identify with his role and find ways to contribute within that position," Kevin says.

"He can move up and down the lineup in effective ways. Not all players can do that. He earned his way up the Boston Bruins team with that capability."

Marchand finished his rookie season sixth in team scoring with 9 goals and 29 points.

The next season the Wildcats brought in former NHL coach Ted Nolan and his long-time assistant Danny Flynn of Nova Scotia. It was a big season for the Wildcats. They were hosting the Memorial Cup and guaranteed a spot in the four-team tournament. The 2005–06 season edition of the Wildcats was highly skilled, with the lineup including future NHLers Keith Yandle, Andrew MacDonald, and Philippe Dupuis.

After a slow start, Marchand began to show he was developing into a junior star. He more than doubled his point total—66—and found the back of the net twenty-nine times. Nolan was impressed. He also saw a future NHLer in his young player.

"He's going to be a dynamite steal," Nolan told the website Futures Hockey that season. "People might say he's too small, but with the way the game's changing, everything's revolving around skill and speed, and Brad Marchand is a perfect prototype for that new era of hockey."

Marchand speaks highly of Nolan and the impact he had on him, both as a player and a person.

"I always loved Teddy," he says in an interview. "The coaches that year really pushed me to the next level and showed me that I had to be a much better player than I already was.

Marchand and teammate Kristopher Letang during the 2006 season with Val-d'Or. Letang has become a star blueliner with the Pittsburgh Penguins. (CREDIT: VAL-D'OR FOREURS)

"They also taught us how to be pros. That's the first real taste I had of it. When you have guys that have been around the NHL, that lifestyle, they kind of brought that to our team. It was a whole different dynamic. It was a really, really big learning experience. It was incredible."

The Wildcats won the QMJHL title that year but endured heartbreak at the Memorial Cup in front of a sold-out crowd at the Moncton Coliseum, losing in the final to Patrick Roy and the Quebec Remparts.

That off-season, the now-rebuilding Wildcats traded Marchand to the Val-d'Or

Marchand on ice with Val-d'Or in the QMJHL. (CREDIT: VAL-D'OR FOREURS)

When Marchand knew Val-d'Or was going to trade him, he asked to go to Halifax. (CREDIT: VAL-D'OR FOREURS)

Foreurs where he spent the next season and a half in the northern Quebec town, located about six hours from Montreal. It was with Val-d'Or that Marchand first made the Canadian junior team, and captured his first of two gold medals.

A Christmas–time trade during the 2007–08 season saw him dealt from Val-d'Or to the team he grew up watching and idolizing: the Halifax Mooseheads. Marchand knew, at nineteen, that this was in all likelihood his last year playing junior, and the Foreurs were able to work out a deal with Halifax, one of the top teams in the QMJHL at that time. Val-d'Or was going to move Marchand, and he asked his general manager to see if the Mooseheads were a possibility.

"Even after I got traded, he told me that there was a better trade on the table from another team, but we respect you and your wish to want to play back home," Marchand says. "I was very, very grateful for that."

There would be no Hollywood ending to this story. For whatever reason, Marchand and the Mooseheads never seemed to gel. He

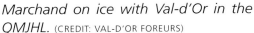

> I was used as a scapegoat, there's no question about it. It was tough to see it go down like that."— Brad Marchand on being a healthy scratch by the Halifax Mooseheads for his last junior game.

posted good numbers—more than a point per game—but fans and team brass were hungry for more from a player who had just won a second gold medal for Canada at the world juniors and was almost anointed as the final piece to Halifax's dream of a first QMJHL title.

In the post season, Halifax made it to the third round against Gatineau Olympiques and Marchand's fellow NHL star Claude Giroux. The Mooseheads were the favourites going into the series, but began a meltdown that saw them lose the first three games, including two at home. They were suddenly facing a do-or-die situation heading into game four, the biggest game of the season.

That's when Marchand says he was blindsided. The Mooseheads told him, after getting off the team bus for the game in Gatineau, that he wasn't playing. Marchand was shocked. His parents were devastated. Halifax would end up losing game four and Marchand watched a remarkable junior career end while sitting in the stands, wearing a suit as a healthy scratch.

"I was used as a scapegoat, there's no question about it. It was tough to see it go down like that," Marchand says, obviously still holding bitterness towards the organization.

Marchand joined two of his best friends in Halifax—Andrew Bodnarchuk and Ryan Hillier, a draft pick of the New York Rangers the same year. Bodnarchuk was the team captain and says he had no insight into why the team sat his friend in game four against Gatineau, but remembers wondering what was going on.

"I think it was an unfair stain on Brad's career at the time," he says. "There were a lot of unnecessary questions coming out about his character. I know Boston was calling Halifax to find out what happened."

Play-by-play man Dan Roberston was calling the Mooseheads games for Eastlink TV that season. Robertson, now the radio voice for the Montreal Canadiens for TSN, admits to not knowing the ins and outs of why Marchand sat, but believes the Mooseheads had their reasons.

"If Cam Russell [then head coach] sits you in games of that importance, I'm siding with Cam. If he was acting the right way, he would have played."

He also noticed that Marchand and the Mooseheads never seemed to mesh.

"Sometimes a guy doesn't fit," he says.

Marchand playing for the Halifax Mooseheads in the QMJHL. (CREDIT: MIKE DEMBECK)

"There's nothing that happened to cause the situation. When I went to talk to the coach, he told me to talk to the general manager. It was his call. When I went to talk to the general manager, I was told it was the owner's call. When I went to talk to the owner, I was told it was the coach's call. No one wanted to own up to it and I wasn't given an explanation about why I wasn't playing.

"It would have been nice to be dealt with as a human, as a man, as a professional."

This wasn't just about not playing a game for Marchand and his family. His reputation was put into question and the Bruins—who had drafted him two years earlier—wondered what was going on. Boston even kept Marchand home after the Mooseheads playoffs while other top-level picks for the Bruins, including Bodnarchuk, joined the team's American Hockey League affiliate in Providence, Rhode Island.

"It almost had a huge impact on my career. It was the first thing [the Bruins] spoke to me about when I showed up at camp—what happened the year before," says Marchand, who also had questions about his attitude surface when playing for Canada at the world juniors.

QMJHL STATISTICS

- 2004–05: Moncton Wildcats – 61 GP, 9G, 20A, 29P
- 2005–06: Moncton Wildcats – 68 GP, 29G, 37A, 66P
- 2006–07: Val-d'Or Foreurs – 57 GP, 33G, 47A, 80P
- 2007–08: Val-d'Or Foreurs – 33GP, 21G, 23A, 44P
- 2007–08: Halifax Mooseheads – 6GP, 10G, 19A, 29P

His father takes it a step further when talking about the Mooseheads and their decision to sit him in that game four, which he refers to as a "scapegoat routine."

"It actually held him back a whole year. That choice [by the Mooseheads] put him back in the AHL for a year because they wanted to understand what happened," Kevin says. "What is the problem? What happened? It raises question marks. They want to understand internally how he responds to coaching, how disciplined is he. But it held him back a year. I hold the Mooseheads accountable for a year's salary."

A sad ending. But many good days in hockey lay ahead.

A BRUIN IS BORN

GOING INTO THE 2006 NHL DRAFT at General Motors Place in Vancouver, the seats were filled with many of the top draft-eligible players and their families. One family not there was the Marchands. After a great season with the Wildcats, Marchand was considered a safe bet to get drafted, but his family knew he wasn't going in the first round. So Kevin kept his son at home.

"I just don't believe that you should go up there and wait in that environment and watch twenty or thirty other kids be paraded across that stage, and you watch them and to think for one moment they are superior to you," he says in giving his reasons as to why. "It's a bit of an internal pride that, and I don't want that to belittle him."

It's also why Kevin didn't take Brad to the QMJHL draft two years earlier. He couldn't get a guarantee his son would go in the first round, so they stayed home.

"It's one of those things. You are weighing what are you missing out on, what are you gaining from the experience. I've heard

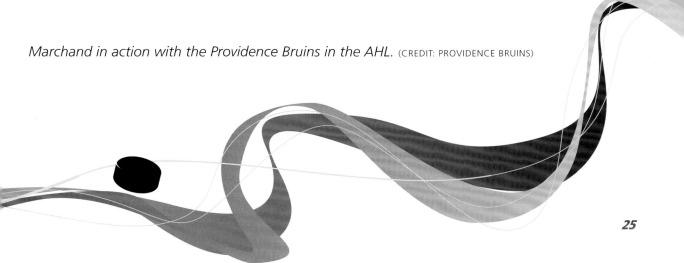

Marchand in action with the Providence Bruins in the AHL. (CREDIT: PROVIDENCE BRUINS)

BOSTON BRUINS NHL DRAFT PICKS 2006

- 5. Phil Kessel (RW)
- 37. Yuri Alexandrov (D)
- 50. Milan Lucic (LW)
- 71. Brad Marchand (LW)
- 128. Andrew Bodnarchuk (D)
- 158. Levi Nelson (C)

TOP NHL DRAFT PICKS 2006

1. Erik Johnson, St. Louis Blues
2. Jordan Staal, Pittsburgh Penguins
3. Jonathan Toews, Chicago Blackhawks
4. Nicklas Bäckström, Washington Capitals
5. Phil Kessel, Boston Bruins
6. Derick Brassard, Columbus Blue Jackets
7. Kyle Okposo, New York Islanders
8. Peter Mueller, Phoenix Coyotes
9. James Sheppard, Minnesota Wild
10. Michael Frolík, Florida Panthers

Don Cherry talk about the kids who sit in the stands and who thought they'd be selected, and they're sitting there and are deflated because their position wasn't predicted," he goes on to say.

"That kind of stuck with me. You don't ever want to think you're less than that opponent—whether they're on the team you're with or otherwise, don't ever allow yourself to feel that second-best-type attitude."

Instead of being in Vancouver, Marchand's family and friends watched the proceedings take place online from their Hammonds Plains home.

Kevin was ready for his son to go anywhere. "I tried to buy every jersey in the league and every hat," he laughs.

The highs and lows were evident that day. Knowing Boston had interest in him, Marchand thought the number-fifty pick—a late second-round selection—might be him. It wasn't. Milan Lucic—all six foot four and 235 pounds of him—was taken instead.

"There was Brad's spot right there. That's the spot he wanted," Kevin remembers. "He was devastated at that moment. For twenty-one more picks, he was devastated."

Boston had another chance to get Marchand in the third round. This time, his name was called. The party was on at the Marchand household.

"We didn't know what round or what team. It was nerve-racking," Lynn says of the day.

Getting drafted is one thing. Making it to the NHL is another. Family friend and former Bruins scout, the late Donnie Matheson, came for a barbecue that summer to meet with Marchand and Bodnarchuk, also taken by Boston in the fifth round. Marchand would have two more years of junior before he'd become a professional, Matheson predicted. And then, there was more work to do.

"Expect to be at least two years in the AHL," Kevin remembers Matheson telling them. "He was bang on. It set our goals, it set our awareness."

Even after the disappointment of sitting out that last game with Halifax, Marchand had done everything he could in junior, and knew he'd be moving up to play in the Bruins farm system. However, the cloud of sitting out that last game carried into the Bruins training camp for the 2007–08 season.

"There was a big black mark on my record," Marchand says.

Marchand was a top point producer for the Providence Bruins in the AHL.
(CREDIT: PROVIDENCE BRUINS)

Marchand had to prove the things people were saying about him and a possible attitude problem weren't true. As expected, Boston sent the twenty year old to the American Hockey League and he suited up for the Providence Bruins for the entire 2008–09 season.

In an interview with *Metro Halifax* in 2009, then Providence Bruins head coach Rob Murray told the publication Marchand had an unusual request for him during his rookie year: "He came in early in the season and said, 'I want you to make me a man as a hockey player,'" Murray said.

Murray also spoke about how he gave his then young forward a "clean slate" as a hockey player when he joined the team, and that his game was elevating at the professional level.

"He's done everything I've asked," Murray told *Metro*. "I can give it to him. He comes off the ice and if he's done something I don't like, I let him know. He's thick-skinned. He doesn't pout."

"I just had to show I was maturing and learning from past experiences," Marchand says about trying to getting back on the Bruins's good side. "It was to grow and learn from something you didn't know of. But I just went in and tried to have a clean slate. I just tried to keep out of any trouble and play the game, work hard, and show them that I was trying to improve every day."

Brad Marchand Career American Hockey League statistics

- 2007–08: Providence Bruins – 79GP, 18G, 41A, 59P
- 2008–09: Providence Bruins – 34GP, 13G, 19A, 32P

Marchand enjoyed a stellar rookie season, recording 18 goals, 41 assists, and a plus-13 rating. He also won the team's rookie-of-the-year award and was showing the Bruins he could be an impact pro player.

"He got up there and once again worked really hard, set his mind to being the best that he could be," Kevin says. "He always tried to be better that everyone— whether they were on his team or off his team, because they were all still his competition. It's the toughest thing to be. Being on a team, working within a team, but then competing against players on your team for those positions."

Looking back now, Marchand was happy to have spent that entire season in Providence. He was learning the pro game and it helped him later appreciate the life he now lives.

"I think it's great for everyone to get a taste of the minors, see what it's like down there," he says. "When you're bussing all night long to a game or playing three games in three nights—that stuff is hard on the body.

"When you go through everything in the minors—when you have some tough days, some ups and downs—it's just so nice to really appreciate how lucky and fortunate we are to be in the position we are in."

MAKING
THE BRUINS

MARCHAND WAS SHOWING REAL improvement heading into the Bruins 2009–10 training camp, but was sent down to Providence again. This second pro season, however, would be very different.

Boston ran into injury trouble, and Marchand was called up and played in twenty games over the course of the season. His NHL debut came in Boston against the Nashville Predators on October 21, 2009—less than two years after finishing junior. He didn't score that game. In fact, he only finished with one assist over the twenty games in Boston, but it set the stage for his next season and landing a full-time spot.

"I kind of had an idea it was coming. I was playing pretty well…They told me to be ready," he says of that first NHL game. "It makes all your dreams come true, that one moment—all the hard work pays off."

When Marchand found out he made the Bruins his next season he was thrilled, but he and his parents knew he couldn't take his foot off the gas or he'd be right back down in the

Marchand started to show that he could be an impact player when he was in the American Hockey League. He just needed to stay out of trouble. (CREDIT: PROVIDENCE BRUINS)

How high was Brad Marchand on his coach in Boston? Well to this day he considers Claude Julien one of the NHL's all-time best. So it wasn't easy later in his career when the only coach he knew in the NHL was fired in February 2017.

The underachieving Bruins were in the midst of a tailspin and team brass decided to act. Like he always does, Marchand spoke from the heart when talking to reporters about the team's decision that day.

"It's difficult. It's something that we kind of brought upon ourselves. We didn't perform the way that we should and that we're capable of. Claude is taking the fall for that. Claude is an incredible coach and he has been for a long time. He's won everything, I think, that you can win," Marchand is quoted as saying by NBC Sports after the firing.

"We have a tremendous amount of respect for him in this room and we were fortunate to have him as long as we did. I learned a ton from him, and I can easily say I wouldn't be the same player if he wasn't my coach for the last number of years. It's very disappointing and frustrating because this was avoidable if we had all done our jobs."

minors. Adding to the anxiety was an injury to veteran Bruins forward Marco Sturm at training camp. Kevin wondered if his son's spot on Boston would be a temporary one.

"We were excited he made the team but we were still nervous because we knew there were injured players. And what happens when he comes back?" he says, in reference to Sturm.

Marchand was also off to a slow start out the gates points-wise. He was creating chances but couldn't bury them. He went the first six weeks without a goal.

"He was trying to find ways to be positive. He was contributing. He was hitting posts. He was just shooting wide on breakaways. He was so close. He could have had fifteen points," Kevin says.

Finally, that elusive first NHL goal came. Facing the Sabres in Buffalo on November 3, 2010, the Bruins were short-handed and Marchand was in behind the defence at his own blue line. He grabbed a loose puck and showcased his speed by breaking in all alone on goaltender Jhonas Enroth. He then looked and fired a perfect shot far-blocker side.

His teammates swarmed him after the game's first tally. Marchand skated to the bench and couldn't wipe the smile off his face.

Marchand doesn't just have style and flare on the ice.

Off the ice, he gets noticed too.

In 2011, Marchand was named to a list of the twenty-five most stylish Bostonians by the *Boston Globe*.

Marchand likes to look his best on game days, and even nights on the town. But his teammates at the time were stunned to learn that Number 63 was named to such a list.

According to the New England Sports Network, Nathan Horton claimed there must have been a printing error. Tough guy Shawn Thornton took it a step further, chalking it up, "as an indication that Bostonians consider shirtless with a shaved chest to be 'stylish,'" the NESN story said.

For the list, Marchand was asked by the *Globe* to describe his personal style.

"Most of the time, if I see something I like, I'll try it on," he offered. "And then, you know, I'll see different styles in movies and stuff."

Marchand and Andrew Bodnarchuk while both playing for the Providence Bruins in the AHL. (CREDIT: PROVIDENCE BRUINS)

"I was actually caught out of position," Marchand says. "It just ended up on my stick, and I turned around and was on a breakaway. I think it was like almost thirty games to that point that I hadn't scored. I just remember going in and telling myself to shoot the puck and hit the net. Luckily, it found a hole."

Marchand became a regular point producer after that first marker. Making things even better, a few weeks later the Bruins dealt Sturm to the Los Angeles Kings. The moved sealed the deal. Marchand was in the NHL for good.

TOP–SCORING LEADERS FOR NHL ROOKIES (2010–11) FROM NHL.COM.

1. Jeff Skinner, Carolina: 31G, 32A, 63P

2. Logan Couture, San Jose: 32G, 24A, 56P

3. Michael Grabner, New York Islanders: 34G, 18A, 52P

4. Tyler Ennis, Buffalo: 20G, 29A, 49P

5. Derek Stepan, New York Rangers: 21G, 24A, 45P

T-6. Jordan Eberle, Edmonton: 18G, 25A, 43P

T-6. Kevin Shattenkirk, St. Louis/Colorado: 9G, 33A, 43P

8. Taylor Hall, Edmonton: 22G, 20A, 42P

9. Brad Marchand, Boston: 21G, 20A, 41P

10. Cam Fowler, Anaheim: 10G, 30A, 40P

"When [Sturm] was ready to come back and they traded him, that showed then that Brad was going to be permanently on that team," Kevin says.

Marchand went on to record 21 goals, 20 assists, and, maybe most impressively, a plus-25 rating (which means he was on the ice for 25 more goals than were scored against his team). He was playing a regular shift and found a place on the second line with Patrice Bergeron and Mark Recchi.

Anyone who ever thought Marchand wouldn't make it as a NHLer was now seeing first-hand just how wrong they were.

Marchand says, "A lot of it in this league goes with opportunity. And I was given the opportunity."

That opportunity came from then Bruins head coach Claude Julien. The two were close, but Julien was hard on his up-and-coming star. He held him very accountable.

"I think we had more meetings in one year than the rest of the team combined, in the ten years I've been here," Marchand says laughing. "He really made a big effort to work with me. He was hard on me at times, but it's because he expected a lot out of me, and I wouldn't have had it any other way."

His father remembers a story Marchand told him prior to his rookie season. Julien told his young forward he wanted ten goals from him for the year. Marchand's response: "I'll get you twenty."

"That's the level of confidence he had," Kevin says. "It's kind of like those training wheels."

Julien believed in him, and Marchand didn't want to let him down.

"There are a lot of coaches in this league who would've had me on the third or fourth line and kept me there," Marchand says. "He really pushed me. I think he saw something in me that I could be a better player, and he was all over me for it."

His successful rookie regular season was only the beginning. The best was still to come for Marchand in the playoffs.

STANLEY CUP CHAMPION

THE BRUINS WENT INTO THE 2011 playoffs as the third-ranked team from the Eastern Conference. They opened the playoffs against their archrival, the Montreal Canadiens, who came in at number six. The teams went at it tooth and nail, with the Bruins pulling it out in overtime in a deciding game seven at TD Garden in Boston.

Marchand's superstitions were coming out, too, during the series. Every time his mother went to a game against Montreal, the Bruins lost. So after game six, Marchand took action.

"He came out [of the dressing room] and said, 'Mom, I don't want to be rude, but you can't come to any more games,'" Lynn recalls. The rule was she could only watch her son live again when the team lost. They won the next five games, including a second-round series sweep of the Philadelphia Flyers.

"He was polite about it, but he was very superstitious," Lynn says. "So I lost the whole next series. They just kept winning and winning."

After beating the Tampa Bay Lightning in another hard-fought seven-game series,

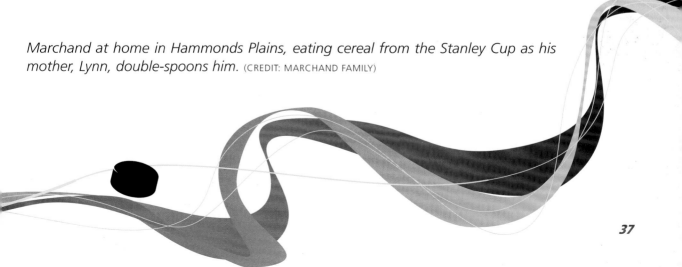

Marchand at home in Hammonds Plains, eating cereal from the Stanley Cup as his mother, Lynn, double-spoons him. (CREDIT: MARCHAND FAMILY)

Boston Bruins's Marchand embracing his parents, Kevin and Lynn, on ice.

(CREDIT: MARCHAND FAMILY)

Marchand's incredible playoff performance was a record-breaking one. His 11 goals were a rookie playoff record for the NHL. He also had 8 assists to finish third in team scoring and sixth overall in the league.

His name was also strongly considered for MVP of the playoffs.

All this from a guy who came out of training camp wondering if he would even be on the Bruins roster.

"I have always wanted to be that guy," he says. "I was brought up to want to be the best and be the hero, the winner. I think that's a big part of it. It's just the way I was always taught to play the game."

Marchand and the Bruins were off to the Stanley Cup final. If hockey fans didn't know Marchand before the Cup final, they knew him afterwards. Points, energy, and of course, a thorn in the sides of the Canucks' best players, Marchand did it all in what was a dramatic seven-game series.

A moment that stands out to Kevin came after the Bruins tied the series 2–2, and he and his wife travelled to Vancouver for game five. The series was a vicious one and many expected the referees to clamp down on the rough stuff happening on the ice. Marchand, not one to shy away from after-the-whistle shenanigans, had been told by both his coaches and his parents to take it easy. As a result, Marchand felt stifled in game five. The referees though didn't call the game differently, and Boston was pushed around in a 1–0 setback.

Marchand brings the Stanley Cup home to Hammonds Plains and celebrates with his father, Kevin, and brother, Jeff. (CREDIT: MARCHAND FAMILY)

"He came off the ice and said, 'Sorry, guys, I don't want to talk,'" Kevin recalls. "He walked off to the dressing room. That was it. I don't even think he said that many words to us."

Backs against the wall and back in Boston, the Bruins won game six decisively, 5–2. It was Marchand who gave his team an early lift, opening the scoring five minutes in by firing a perfect wrist shot top-corner over the glove of Vancouver netminder Roberto Luongo.

Boston was now riding a wave of emotion back to Vancouver for game seven. What a night it turned out to be for the Hammonds Plains star. Marchand found Bergeron in front of the Canucks goal with five minutes left in the first period and he made no mistake. 1–0 Boston.

Parents Kevin and Lynn get to hold the Stanley Cup at home. (CREDIT: MARCHAND FAMILY)

Marchand was at it again midway through the second. After good work along the boards, he picked up a loose puck behind the net and scored on a backhanded wrap-around. 2–0 Boston.

Then with Boston up 3–0 late in the third—the final dagger. Marchand broke in on an odd-man rush and scored into the empty net.

The Bruins had done it. Marchand had done it. He was a Stanley Cup champion.

"Somehow in the whole sea of people, he knew where we were. After he scored that [last] goal, he skated over and pointed up at us with excitement," Lynn says proudly, remembering seeing her son from their lower-bowl seats.

"That was just so heartwarming for me that he wanted to celebrate that with us. He was just so happy that we were there to be a part of it all."

Marchand's game-seven heroics showed again how he thrives in the big moments. He was the best player on the ice, recording two goals and an assist.

"I don't think there are many moments that will beat that last game," Marchand says. "That was just incredible, the way that all came together. Even the whole day before the game—the way I felt and the adrenalin rush. Just realizing everything you worked your whole life for came down to one game. I'll never be able to explain that experience, or duplicate it. It was incredible."

A Stanley Cup champion after just turning twenty-three, Marchand spent the next few months enjoying the fruits of his labour. He partied—a lot. And some of those exploits were making the rounds on social media, including a photo of him shirtless dancing at a bar. Marchand makes no apologies for having all the fun that he did that off-season.

"When you win the Stanley Cup at that age, and you basically accomplish your lifelong dream…I'm a little disappointed I didn't celebrate more than I did, because I celebrated a lot," he says candidly.

"There wasn't one thing that could've bothered me at that time. I had no cares about what was going on. The only thing I cared about was that we just won the Cup. That's the only thing that mattered to me, and I was going to celebrate… Again, I wish I could've made it last a lot longer."

Lynn says winning the Cup at such a young age was a lot for him to handle, and his immaturity showed.

"Brad said he was going to party for days. And that's what he did. He was young and immature, and partied a little too hard. There are some pictures out there—like Brad shirtless, dancing on the stage. He didn't know how to control his emotions. He didn't know how to handle it," she says.

Adds Kevin: "He gets very emotional— both highs and lows. He can reach higher levels of emotions and excitement. When he gets excited like that, he lets loose."

LEADING SCORERS FROM 2011 STANLEY CUP PLAYOFFS

- David Krejci, Boston: 12G, 11A, 23P
- Henrik Sedin, Vancouver: 3G, 19A, 22P
- Martin St. Louis, Tampa Bay: 10G, 10A, 20P
- Daniel Sedin, Vancouver: 9G, 11A, 20P
- Patrice Bergeron, Boston: 6G, 14A, 20P
- Brad Marchand, Boston: 11G, 8A, 19P

The best day for the family that summer was when Brad had his day with the Cup. His twenty-four hours included a parade in Halifax followed by a public celebration in Hammonds Plains.

"I don't think anyone slept that night," Lynn says of the party at their home afterwards.

Marchand says being able to bring the Cup to his hometown was an awesome experience that just flew by.

"You just wish you could have spent so much time with it. You want to stop time and be in that moment forever," he says.

THE HATERS

THE HOCKEY WORLD WITNESSED more than simply Marchand's skill set during the 2011 Stanley Cup playoffs. They also saw his antagonizing style front and centre—a role he developed in minor hockey and played to perfection throughout the playoffs.

Two great examples came in that final series against the Canucks.

With Boston enjoying a comfortable third-period lead in game four, the Canucks became enraged after Marchand clotheslined defenceman Christian Ehrhoff in the corner, then went dangerously low and submarined Vancouver forward Daniel Sedin immediately afterwards into the boards. Marchand was penalized and threw off his gloves as several Canucks came after him.

Marchand was up to more tricks late in game six with Boston ahead again and set to send the series back to Vancouver for the deciding game seven. A scrum broke out in front of the Vancouver net, and Marchand

Marchand in a characteristic pose while playing for the Providence Bruins. Marchand is almost as disliked by fans outside Boston as he is loved by Bruins fans.
(CREDIT: MARCHAND FAMILY)

Even the then-president of the United States couldn't resist directing a shot his way.

During the Bruins' visit to The White House after winning the Stanley Cup in 2012, Barack Obama—a well-known Chicago Blackhawks fan—piped up on the play of Brad Marchand, who stood out of camera range in the far corner of the front row, not knowing he'd suddenly see the spotlight put on him.

"Brad Marchand went into the season playing on the fourth line, but the Little Ball of Hate shrugged off the rookie jitters," Obama said while praising the Bruins.

The president then searched him out, much to the laughter of his Boston teammates.

"What's up with that nickname, man?" Obama wondered, looking his way.

"It completely threw me off guard," Marchand says, reflecting back to that day. "To be honest, I was looking around the room, taking it all in. It was such a cool experience.

"I couldn't even hear what he said the first time. I just heard my name. I looked at him. I couldn't believe it. It was so surreal. The president kind of acknowledging you—it's a pretty incredible feeling and one I'll definitely always remember."

gave about ten jabs to the face of Vancouver captain Daniel Sedin, grinning at him by the time the referee finally intervened.

It's antics like this that have endeared him to Boston fans but made him enemy number one by many opposing teams and their supporters.

Dirty, rat, agitator, greasy, pest—all are words used to describe his play since coming into the NHL. Fans even hold up signs in the stand: Exterminate the Rat.

"He doesn't mind being the villain. He likes being the villain," says Dan Roberston, who is from New Glasgow, Nova Scotia, and is one of the best play-by-play hockey voices in the business. "I think that drives him a lot."

Marchand, for his part, seems immune to what people think of him. If anything, he soaks up the attention.

"I love that people hate me," he says. "I know I'm loved in Boston and loved by Bruins fans—that's all that matters. As long as my teammates like me and management likes me and keeps me around, I'm happy.

"I think it's funny and I enjoy it when the fans get upset," he goes on to say. "It's part of the game. I take enjoyment out of it. The more they hate me the more I love it."

Sometimes, he takes it too far. Like once, at the age of fourteen in minor hockey, he got sick of being hooked skating up the ice, so he turned around and two-handed his opponent—with his stick—across the face mask.

"The guy's cage was just mangled," his friend and former minor-hockey teammate Ryan Hillier told the *National Post* in an interview from 2016. "That was the first time when we were like, 'Oh my god, what did we just see?'"

More recently during the 2017–18 season, Marchand was given a five-game suspension for an elbow to the head of an unsuspecting Marcus Johansson of the New Jersey Devils. The two were battling in front of the New Jersey net when Marchand stuck out his right elbow and hit him with a cheap shot.

"I kind of taught my kids, an eye for an eye," Kevin says of his son's hockey mentality. "If someone sticks you, you give it back to them. You don't just give it to him that hard, you give it to him twice as hard…you punish them twice as hard back. So it's a philosophy we've grown up with."

And of course, there are the now-infamous licking incidents from the 2018 playoffs. Marchand first licked the face of Leo Komarov of the Toronto Maple Leafs in the first round, then did it again to Tampa Bay Lightning forward Ryan Callahan in round two—a series Boston went on to lose. The incidents drew the ire of many around hockey and resulted in Marchand being "put on notice" by the league to stop a behaviour many felt was disgusting. The Bruins forward later admitted he had gone too far.

> My mom likes to say that I came out of the womb 'mischievous,'" Marchand, 2018 article on The Players' Tribune.

"I think the biggest thing for me now is to really take a pretty hard look in the mirror and realize that some of the things I'm doing have much bigger consequences than I may ever think or really believe will come out of it," Marchand told reporters in May 2018 after the Boston players were cleaning out their lockers for the season after being eliminated in the playoffs.

"The last thing I ever want to do is bring the embarrassment on my teammates and the organization that it did. I have to be a lot better. I know I've said that in the past, but I think that's going to be the thing that I really work on the most. I think I've kind of gotten my game to a pretty decent spot, but I've got some character things and things that I've done that clearly need some fixing."

Marchand doesn't see himself as a dirty player, however. What he concedes to is "crossing the line a little more than some other players."

"But I also have a bigger microscope on me, or a lot more people watching me because of the way that I play," he fires back when being interviewed for this book. "So every time that I cross the line, it gets blown up a lot because I have a prior history. Again, it's part of the game and it always will be. I don't know if I'll ever get it out of my game—I'm going to try—but it happens so quick in hockey."

Marchand's father says his son uses his style to get more separation from the puck. But it can cause some sleepless nights for the parents.

"I'm always fearful that if you antagonize too many guys, sooner or later someone is going to clock you and hurt you," Kevin says. "So from a parental point of view, I'm always concerned about safety."

Adds Lynn: "Sometimes he can't keep his emotions in check, and that gets him in trouble."

Hockey fans generate most of their hate towards Marchand on social media sites like Twitter and Facebook. If he does something dirty, the haters come out in force, and come at him using strong language. Even when he does nothing wrong in a game—which is more times than not—his past indiscretions always seem to pop back up.

"Where all the hate is coming from is because I am successful at what I do," Marchand says. "It's a compliment when people don't like me or my game, because it means I'm doing something… I mean, I'm fortunate to be a part of a great organization and be in the NHL. I may play in a way that people don't like, but it's noticed because I'm in the NHL. I'm enjoying it, I love it. I always will."

"He just shakes it off," Lynn says of the verbal attacks. "When the negative comments still keep coming, it might bother him a bit, but he'd like to leave that early perception people have of him, behind him."

Marchand is working towards that, but it's not easy. He needs to play close to that edge to be the successful NHL player he's become. But there's consensus in his inner circle that he should eliminate the dirty hits that lead to suspensions. They hurt his reputation, and more importantly, his team, as the Bruins are counting on him night in and night out.

Brad Marchand shares a laugh with NHL superstar Sidney Crosby of the Pittsburgh Penguins during the All-Stars Game weekend in Tampa, Florida, in January 2018.

AN NHL SUPERSTAR

THE NUMBERS DON'T LIE IN showing how good Marchand has become. Eight full seasons in the NHL and in seven of them, 20 or more goals. Three times he has found the back of the net 30-plus times, including 39 during the 2016–17 season. That same year he also had a career-high 85 points—superb by today's NHL standards.

But that's just his offensive side. Defensively, he's one of the top penalty killers in the league. He is also always amongst the leaders for short-handed goals, and in six of eight seasons, has recorded a plus-minus rating of at least plus-20. Not bad for a guy many thought wasn't good enough to play in the league.

"I don't think a lot of people did," Marchand says of where he is now. "It goes back to—I guess, my father, my family always telling me I could and push me to go to that next level."

In the first two rounds of the 2006 NHL draft, team after team bypassed Marchand for players who ended up becoming NHL busts.

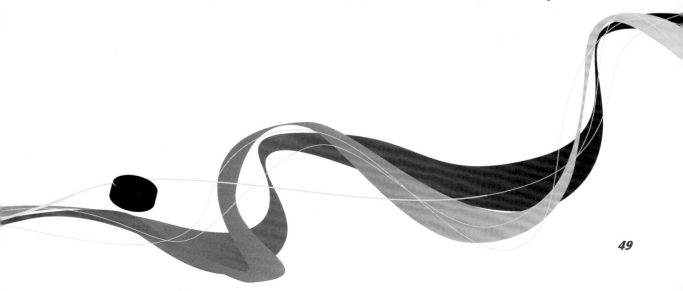

Brad Marchand loves the big moments. The bigger the game, the bigger the spotlight, and the better he seems to play.

Fans saw that in the 2011 Stanley Cup final against the Vancouver Canucks, and it's continued throughout his NHL career.

"I have always wanted to be *that guy*," Marchand says. "I was brought up to want to be the best and be the hero—the winner. I think that's a big part of it. It's just the way I was always taught to play the game. It's also about confidence. We've all been there before, but I get excited to be in those opportunities, those moments."

This type of swagger isn't everyone's cup of tea. But it works for him and he uses it to be successful.

"People say he's cocky but I say he's confident," Andrew Bodnarchuk says. "He's got a supreme confidence."

and you'll be hard pressed to find a better player from that draft class not named Brad Marchand.

"I don't know how you define what a superstar is, but if it's not him, he's goddamn close," Dan Robertson says. "It's like he gets better every year. He has to be on the short list of the best left wingers in the league."

You will never hear Marchand say he's surprised by how good he's become. Confidence is something he has never lacked and it's helped him get where he is today. He is able to succeed in whatever role he's given, too, and doesn't get intimidated by playing with—or against—the NHL's best.

"Honestly, it's 100 per cent his competitive nature," Bodnarchuk says. "Every year I'm more shocked, as every year he gets better, and you scratch your head. I think it's his ability to never be satisfied with something."

Prior to the 2016–17 season, the Bruins showed Marchand how important he was to the franchise. Boston signed him to an eight-year contract extension worth a whopping $49 million. It works out to an annual salary of $6.125 million through to the 2024–25 season.

"It hasn't changed him," Kevin says of the money he is making. "That's one of the things we work hard on, actually—to keep him grounded and appreciative."

The list includes: goaltender Riki Helenius (one NHL game); blue-liner Ty Wishart (twenty-seven NHL games); centre Tomas Kana (six NHL games); and winger Igor Makarov (no NHL games). In fact, take out names like Jonathan Toews, Nicklas Backstrom, Phil Kessel, and Claude Giroux,

Boston Bruins centre Patrice Bergeron hugs Brad Marchand during a game against the Tampa Bay Lightning in Tampa, Florida, in April 2018. (CHRIS O'MEARA, THE ASSOCIATED PRESS)

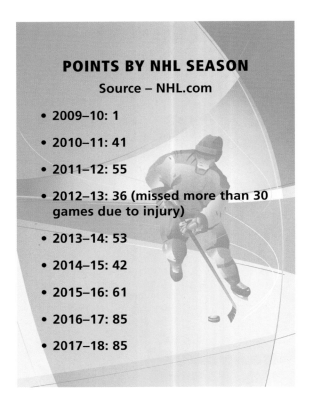

POINTS BY NHL SEASON

Source – NHL.com

- 2009–10: 1
- 2010–11: 41
- 2011–12: 55
- 2012–13: 36 (missed more than 30 games due to injury)
- 2013–14: 53
- 2014–15: 42
- 2015–16: 61
- 2016–17: 85
- 2017–18: 85

It might surprise you to learn Marchand is actually pretty frugal. His father tells the story of how, after his first NHL contract with the Bruins, Marchand purchased a Lamborghini after saving up $1 million. His dad had one rule—you don't get the car until you're twenty-five or you save a million bucks.

"I knew it would take that long [to save it]. And he did; he waited," Kevin says, smiling.

Fast-forward to the next year and that sporty yellow Lamborghini was gone.

Marchand sold it. "He realized that he hardly ever used it and it wasn't a good investment," Kevin says of why he parted ways with it.

"He's still very cautious on how he does spend his money," Lynn adds. "He enjoys living the good life, but he's also cautious of how he spends it."

Marchand talks a lot about "opportunity" getting him where he is today. And one of the biggest was when the Bruins lined him up alongside one of the league's best: Patrice Bergeron. The Edmonton Oilers of the 1980s had Wayne Gretzky and Jari Kurri. The St. Louis Blues of the 1990s had Brett Hull and Adam Oates. From 2011 and beyond, the Bruins have had Marchand and Bergeron. Right from the get-go, the two clicked and continue to form one of the league's best forward duos.

"When you play with that guy like that, you have to play to his standards too," Marchand says of Bergeron. "I think that's a big part of why I began playing like I did because he's such an incredible player—such an all-star—you have to play to that level. You are expected to carry your weight if you want to play on that line. He holds his linemates accountable."

Marchand considers Bergeron one of the league's best players and top centremen.

The two don't just play a regular shift together—they also kill penalties and skate on the same power-play unit.

Bergeron is from L'Ancienne-Lorette, Quebec, and also played in the QMJHL from 2001–03 with the Acadie-Bathurst Titan. The centreman quietly goes about his business with little flare, which is the polar opposite of Marchand, yet the tandem has a chemistry few can match.

"I think it's a lot about communication and years," Bergeron said after a game last year in Calgary when Marchand scored the overtime-winning goal in a 2–1 victory. "But right from the get-go, we would see each other well on the ice and finding ways to give each other the puck."

Bergeron is a big Marchand fan and isn't surprised by how good he's become.

"He plays on the edge. He wants the puck and he wants to make an impact," he says. "He'll be the first one to tell you sometimes he does get carried away and goes beyond that, but he's been working really hard to reel that in and play the right way."

Brad Marchand hoists the World Cup following Canada's victory over Team Europe in Toronto on September 29, 2016. (CREDIT: THE CANADIAN PRESS)

O CANADA

BEFORE TALKING ABOUT HIS TWO gold medals for Canada at the IIHF World Junior Hockey Championships or scoring the game-winning goal for his country in the gold-medal game of the World Cup of Hockey, Marchand's father thinks back to the under-18 Canadian team his son tried out for in the summer of 2005.

"It was like a real war on the ice," he remembers. "There was hardly any hockey being played. It was nuts."

Kevin thinks he usually knew, going into any tryout, where his son would stand in terms of making a roster. Not at this camp. The best forty or so under-18 players from across the country were there, and it was basically may the best man win.

"It was honest to God one of the toughest competitions I had ever seen to make a Canadian team. It was absolutely out of his world," Kevin says.

Marchand made the squad and Canada would go on to win gold. His performance at the Under-18 Junior World Cup in Breclav, Czech Republic, and Piestany, Slovakia, opened eyeballs within brass for the Team Canada junior squad.

Marchand after Canada wins gold at World Juniors. (CREDIT: MARCHAND FAMILY)

The goal the next year was to be invited to the team's summer tryout camp. Marchand and his father would set up his off-season training so he would peak when the August tryout rolled around. Marchand was invited, and—like he always does—left an impression.

"When he got on the ice, he was the best player," Kevin says. "He had the best camp. There is only one other player who compared—and I don't know which one was better—and that was Jonathan Toews. They led the ice—up and down. I couldn't believe it. I've never been so proud."

A few months later Marchand was invited back to the December main camp. It became evident quickly that Canada expected him to make the team and play an important role.

"They were slotting him on the top line, with top players, which was phenomenal,"

The World Cup of Hockey marked the first high-level competition where Brad Marchand played on the same team with fellow Nova Scotian Sidney Crosby. The two have skated together in the off-season, but it surprised many to see how well the two gelled at the tournament.

"Their chemistry matched each other," says Kevin. "It's like the boys were buddies off the ice and buddies on the ice."

The 2016 event also marked the first real opportunity the Marchands had to meet the Crosby family, including Sidney's parents, Troy and Trina. It was a great experience for everyone.

"There's a lot of attention around Sidney…and when a team's doing well, and Sidney's doing well, you don't change things too much," Kevin adds.

If there is one check left for Marchand internationally, it would to play for Canada at the Olympics. He would've been a strong contender to make it had NHL players gone to the PyeongChang Winter Games in 2018. Given his track

World Junior team headshot.
(CREDIT: MARCHAND FAMILY)

record for winning gold medals, he'll do so again if NHL players return to the Olympics in 2022.

"We haven't really felt the blow of it not working," Lynn says of her son's success at big international events. "I never want to lose."

Marchand being interviewed after winning a gold medal for Canada at World Juniors. Marchand was a favourite interviewee by many media members at the event. (CREDIT: MARCHAND FAMILY)

his father says. "That's when I could start seeing how Brad could fit into the NHL."

Over the next two years, Marchand helped Canada win two gold medals at the prestigious event, which draws the biggest TV hockey audience next to the Stanley Cup playoffs. He finished the two years with 6 international goals, including 4 at the 2008 tournament when he felt he played better and was proving his worth.

"He was getting national exposure. He was scoring some big goals. It was a phenomenal time for us," Kevin says. "He was used in a lot of the commercials. We loved seeing Brad associated with Team Canada. It's a sense of pride for all of us—a huge sense of pride."

Marchand's time with the junior program wasn't all rosy. He and head coach Brent Sutter sometimes butted heads, most notably during a 2007 summertime Super Series against Russia. Sutter benched Marchand in the final game of that event,

SCORING LEADERS 2016 WORLD CUP

Player	Team	GP	G	A	Pts	+/-
Sidney Crosby	Canada	6	3	7	10	8
Brad Marchand	Canada	6	5	3	8	5
Patrice Bergeron	Canada	6	4	3	7	4
Jonathan Toews	Canada	6	3	2	5	6
Matt Duchene	Canada	6	2	2	4	3
Johnny Gaudreau	N America	3	2	2	4	2
Nicklas Backstrom	Sweden	3	2	2	4	3
John Tavares	Canada	4	2	2	4	3

Source: WCH2016

calling him out publicly to clean up his act. Marchand was quoted afterwards about himself at the tournament as having "a real attitude problem before," and not being the person "he had to be off the ice."

After world juniors, Marchand next played for Canada at the IIHF World Hockey Championships in the spring of 2016 when Boston didn't make the play-offs. Again, it was a golden moment for Marchand, who finished the tournament with 7 points in 10 games as Canada went 9–1 for the event.

Marchand would go on to enjoy his biggest moment on the international stage when he was named to Team Canada for the World Cup of Hockey in September 2016.

To say he played well is an understatement. He was put on the team's top line—with Patrice Bergeron and Sidney Crosby, no less—and led the tournament with 5 goals as Canada came out on top with a dramatic come-from-behind 2–1 victory against Team Europe to sweep the best-of-three final.

And like he always seems to do, Marchand shone the brightest when it

Marchand at the U-18 championships in the Czech Republic. (CREDIT: MARCHAND FAMILY)

mattered most. He potted the game winner short-handed by coming off the bench, catching up to teammate Jonathan Toews, and firing a perfect wrist shot past the blocker of Team Europe goaltender Jaroslav Halak.

After scoring, Marchand jumped several feet in the air before being mobbed by his teammates.

"When I saw him cut to the middle, I saw the opportunity to jump into the open space," Marchand says about that huge goal, which came with 43.1 seconds left in the third period in a 1–1 game. "I just wanted to get a shot off quick. It was pretty unbelievable feeling to watch it go in and know there was only a minute left in the game, especially being short-handed."

Brad Marchand leaps in the air after scoring the winning goal for Team Canada against Team Europe during the World Cup final in Toronto. He is known for his high-stakes goals.
(FRANK GUNN, THE CANADIAN PRESS)

Kevin grins ear to ear thinking about that goal, which he and Lynn watched live at the Air Canada Centre in Toronto.

"It was a great opportunity, but it could go negative," he says of his son making the World Cup team. "It never did. It was a positive experience throughout."

"I think that was just a whole other level," Brad says about the event. "It was the team I really, really wanted to make. I was so proud to be a part of that team. And I didn't think that I would, based on the players that were available, but it was an incredible feeling the whole way through."

OFF THE ICE

EVERYONE NEEDS TIME FOR themselves. For Brad Marchand, that comes in the form of hunting in the great outdoors. It's such a passion for Marchand that he recently bought a property in Colorado specifically for hunting expeditions with family and friends.

"It's just something I always grew up doing with my family—my grandfathers, my father, my brother, my cousins," he says. "It's also the way I feel I get away from everything—away from the game, away from stress of life. I get out in the woods and it's my quiet time, my happy space. It's so relaxing.

"When I'm out in nature, it's almost like I feel I get rejuvenated."

Marchand is making a great home for himself in Boston. In September 2015, he married his long-time girlfriend, Katrina Sloane. Two years later, they welcomed their first child together. Marchand is also stepdad to Katrina's son from a previous relationship. He jokingly calls his life now a "little different" to when he was that twenty-three-year-old partying freely after Boston won its Stanley Cup.

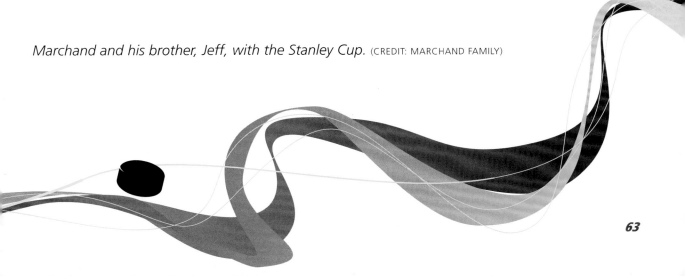

Marchand and his brother, Jeff, with the Stanley Cup. (CREDIT: MARCHAND FAMILY)

GIVING BACK

One of the most heartwarming ways Marchand has given back came after the devastating Boston Marathon bombings. Rocked by the mass devastation and heartbreak, Marchand worked with the Bruins public relations team and auctioned off his luxury suite at TD Garden for the team's first playoff game later that month.

The proceeds went to the family of eight-year-old Martin Richard, who died in the blast. With tickets raffling off for $5 apiece, more than $200,000 was raised for the family. In a diary posted for ESPN titled "Proud to be in Boston" after the bombings, Marchand wrote openly about how the boy's death impacted him.

"A young kid who was a Bruins fan touches everyone's heart," he wrote. "It was very upsetting. Every time you see his picture or hear his name, it brings tears."

The Bruins were the first professional team in the city to play after the bombings. After that game, the players took off their game-worn jerseys and handed them over to first responders who were called to the scene.

"The whole time I was with them they kept thanking me for being a part of everything that was happening, like meeting them and coming to the game," Marchand went on to write in his diary post. "We were sitting there saying, 'No thank *you* for everything you have done. You guys are the heroes.'"

"The older you get, the priorities get situated," he says. "The things I cared about at twenty-two, twenty-three, aren't really important now. I like to spend time with my family and friends, and that's about it. I don't do a whole lot—I focus on my job and my career. When I get some downtime, I spend time with my family. Things have changed."

Boston is a blue-collar town and fans have embraced Marchand's style. The city loves its hockey, especially those who leave it all on the ice like Marchand does. But with that support comes added pressure as they expect him to always be at his best and to keep the Bruins a Stanley Cup contender.

"It's an unbelievable sports town... and they're very vocal about it," he says. "If you are playing good, then you're loved. If you are not, then they're going to get on you. You're expected to pull your weight in this city."

Marchand gets home to Hammonds Plains every off-season for some rest and relaxation. When he does, he looks to give back, whether it be by participating in a local charity event, or stopping to sign an autograph for an admiring fan.

"When I was young, I never thought it was something that came with being

Marchand and his mother at a Stanley Cup celebration. (CREDIT: MARCHAND FAMILY)

in the NHL. I just wanted to play the game. When you get here, you realize the kids do look up to you," he says.

"I remember when I used to look up to the Mooseheads and I met a few of my favourite players when I was younger. Now, I see kids that look up to us, and I remember that feeling."

Andrew Bodnarchuk has noticed his friend maturing and focusing more on his off-ice image. He says Marchand was much more open in the public when he first made the NHL—something he's backed away from in recent years.

"He was more comfortable going to a bar with us, or going to get something to eat. It's not that it was a bad situation—he was just doing things that a regular person that age would do," Bodnarchuk says.

"I think it's fair to say it took him a little while to realize how much in the public eye

Brad Marchand has the NHL's best backhand, according to one hockey analyst. In 2018, Travis Yost, a member of the TSN Hockey Analytics Team, studied how the league's top forwards score. He described Marchand's backhand as "lethal."

"Ten of his goals last year (29.4 per cent) came by way of the backhand, which is the second year in a row he has done that. In fact, in the modern era of the NHL (2007-18), only six players have scored nine or more goals in a single season by way of the backhand. Marchand (in 2011-12, 2015-6, 2016-17, and 2017-18) accounted for four of those. The other two were Corey Perry and Jamie Benn, both in 2010-11."

he was," he goes on to say. "And I don't think he was out of line as a regular teenager… His maturing process was in the public eye. But he's done an amazing job. He's the most humble down-to-earth family guy you'll know now. I think people have a tough time washing the old Brad out of their head at times, but that's passing really quickly now."

Marchand doesn't think money or fame has changed him. The words he uses to describe himself—"outgoing," "vocal," "joking around"—are what you'd expect to hear. He's also easygoing, something you see regularly watching him interact with fans, teammates, and media. He's been known to poke fun at himself, making jokes about his distinctive nose. When some of the Bruins visited a children's hospital in costumes, he went dressed as a rat.

"I feel like I am who you see," he says.

Marchand obliges young fans who ask for retweets. And when a Twitter troll attacked him using a homophobic slur, he struck back: "This derogatory statement is offensive to so many people around the world your [sic] the kind of kid parents are ashamed of." Marchand was happy to be selected as the Bruins's You Can Play ambassador. The program is designed to promote acceptance in NHL dressing rooms, and give potential LGBTQ+ players somebody on their team they can turn to for support.

Kevin and Lynn are very proud of their son and the man he's become. They are seeing their son love where he plays and the team he represents, one of the most beloved in Nova Scotia and the entire NHL. But more importantly, they are seeing their son proudly waving the Hammonds Plains banner and serving his community as a hockey role model.

"Just in how he interacts with people everywhere, especially the kids," Kevin says. "He is really good at supporting the kids, and trying to be a good positive figure by signing autographs, things like that."

Marchand was one of those star-struck youngsters and through hard work and determination is now living the dream of playing in the NHL.

It's been a very fun ride.

Marchand while playing with the Halifax Mooseheads. (CREDIT: MIKE DEMBECK)

APPENDIX

BRAD MARCHAND CAREER STATISTICS												
Year	Team	League	GP	G	A	Pts	PIM	+/-	GP	G	A	Pts	PIM
2004–05	Moncton Wildcats	QMJHL	61	9	20	29	52	0	11	1	0	1	7
2005–06	Moncton Wildcats	QMJHL	68	29	37	66	83	40	20	5	14	19	34
2006–07	Val-d'Or Foreurs	QMJHL	57	33	47	80	108	12	20	16	24	40	36
2007–08	Val-d'Or Foreurs	QMJHL	33	21	23	44	36	-6	--	--	--	--	--
2007–08	Halifax Mooseheads	QMJHL	26	10	19	29	40	8	14	3	16	19	18
2008–09	Providence Bruins	AHL	79	18	41	59	67	13	16	7	8	15	26
2009–10	Providence Bruins	AHL	34	13	19	32	51	14	--	--	--	--	--
2009–10	Boston Bruins	NHL	20	0	1	1	20	-3	--	--	--	--	--
2010–11	Boston Bruins	NHL	77	21	20	41	51	25	25	11	8	19	40
2011–12	Boston Bruins	NHL	76	28	27	55	87	31	7	1	1	2	2
2012–13	Boston Bruins	NHL	45	18	18	36	27	23	22	4	9	13	21
2013–14	Boston Bruins	NHL	82	25	28	53	64	36	12	0	5	5	18
2014–15	Boston Bruins	NHL	77	24	18	42	95	5	--	--	--	--	--
2015–16	Boston Bruins	NHL	77	37	24	61	90	21	--	--	--	--	--
2016–17	Boston Bruins	NHL	80	39	46	85	81	18	6	1	3	4	6
2017–18	Boston Bruins	NHL	68	34	51	85	63	25	12	4	13	17	16
	NHL	TOTALS	602	226	233	459	578						

BRAD MARCHAND INTERNATIONAL PLAY

Year	Age	Team	League	GP	G	A	PTS	+/-	PIM
2006–07	18	Canada	WJC-A	6	2	0	2	2	2
2007–08	19	Canada	WJC-A	7	4	2	6	2	4
2015–16	27	Canada	WC	10	4	3	7	9	10
2016–17	28	Canada	WC	6	5	3	8	5	8

Brad Marchand in the QMJHL. (CREDIT: VAL-D'OR FOREURS)

YOU MAY ALSO ENJOY

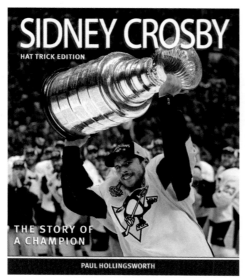

Sidney Crosby
978-1-77108-427-7

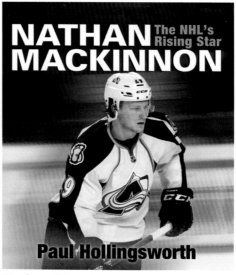

Nathan MacKinnon
978-1-77108-331-7

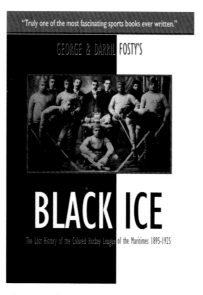

Black Ice: The Lost History of the Colored Hockey League of the Maritimes, 1895–1925
978-1-55109-695-7

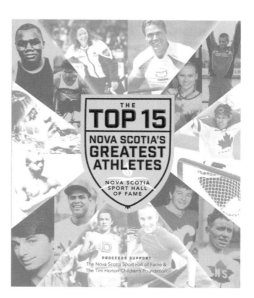

The Top 15: Nova Scotia's Greatest Athletes
978-1-77108-701-8